Our Young Voices

2018

Our Dreams

Cleveland, Ohio

Our Young Voices 2018, *Our Dreams* **© 2018 by Universal Prosperity.**

Co-Contributors:
Amya, Christian, Crieg, D.J., Dewayne, Gregory, Jareese, Kamia, Lawrence, Mikiara, Shanae, Tavonn

For information contact: info@uptownmediaventures.com

Book and Cover design by Team Uptown

ISBN: 978-1-68121-099-5

10 9 8 7 6 5 4 3 2 1

Dedicated to enabling youth the experience of expressing themselves with the written word and the

Pride In Authorship!

Table of Contents

Board Chair Preface

As a retired Director of Public Information for the Cleveland Fire Department, I have been involved in many public service activities that benefit the public at large. I have always had a keen desire to positively influence our youth – the future of our society.

As fortuity would have it, I was presented with the idea of starting an initiative for the benefit of our youth. The initiative, ultimately, became the *Pride in Authorship Initiative*. The folks at a small publishing house, *Uptown Media Joint Ventures*, committed to insure the publication of a semi-annual book called *Our Young Voices.*

After much behind the scenes preparation, I am proud to announce the successful publication of a second volume of *Our Young Voices,* in conjunction with the African American Music Association during the Scholarship Week in conjunction with Infinite Scholars.

This is surely just the beginning and we thank all of our sponsors, supporters, and everyone who has contributed to this extremely worthwhile initiative. So please join us, as we celebrate our young essayists who have earned the right to claim the *Pride in Authorship!*

Larry Gray

Board Chairman, Universal Prosperity, Pride in Authorship Initiative

K Kelly with Winston Gragg, President of the African American Music Association and Member of the Infinite Scholars Board of Directors

Introduction

How many people can claim to be published authors as youths?

The *Our Young Voices* publication is one of the manifestations of the *Pride In Authorship Initiative* that seeks to promote written expression by our youth.

Another part of this initiative is the participation in *Youth Literary and Writing Contests*. The winning essays will be published in the *Our Young Voices* publication, with the winner's photo (if available at printing time), and available on major book retailing web sites like Amazon.com and Barnes & Noble.com. Each winner will receive a free copy of their book, an award certification of authorship, along with other prizes!

Yet, ultimately, the greatest reward is seeing their beaming *Pride In Authorship*!

K Kelly McElroy

Technical Director, Universal Prosperity
CEO, Uptown Media Joint Ventures
Author, Best of the Best, Modern Jazz Recordings; Modern Jazz Classics

Winston Gragg

President African American Music Association and Founder of the Cleveland Scholarship Week

"My idea for being involved with *Our Young Voices* is to make a concentrated effort to helping young people and re-educating adults about today's marketplace. Many adults are afraid of technology, however, our children are not. Walt Disney prepares young children to go to Disney, and we want to prepare kids in elementary and middle school to go to college to get an education. In order to teach young people, you have to get their attention, and that is exactly what *Our Young Voices* is doing."

Dimitrios Kalafatis

Special Events Coordinator
Golden Corral

"Children are our future and I am, personally, proud to support such worthy causes and programs such as Infinite Scholars and the *Our Young Voices* initiative. Golden Corral is committed to the improvement of society-at-large by supporting such noteworthy civic organizations and programs."

Our Dreams Cleveland 2018

EB Smith

M.P.A., Author, Educator
Media Associate for the
African American Music Association
Vice President, E.B. Smith Project LLC

"Higher education helps develop a person's inner gifts. Student's minds are sharpened with the knowledge and critical thinking skills necessary to compete. I am pleased to be involved with the African American Music Association of Cleveland, Ohio and their continued effort in providing access for young people to get to college. I also support the efforts of *Our Young Voices* in promoting literary expression among our youth. My life serves as proof that their life will be better with it."

Jean Wilson

Executive Administrator
African American Music Association

"*Our Young Voices* gives children and teens an opportunity to express their idea in a public forum. It teaches them how to communicate both written and verbally. Developing these skills at an early age also helps young people to build high self-esteem as well as interpersonal (dealing with others) and intrapersonal communication skills. Students also learn key competencies such as: the ability to solve problems, how to control thoughts and actions, use of critical thinking skills, and the ability to motivate others. We are really excited about the *Our Young Voices* program, because it is making a difference in young people's lives."

Endorsements

Russell Atkins

Carol Shaheed

Judy Jackson-Winston

Harry Boomer

Vince Robinson

Russell Atkins

(Russell Atkins wearing Cleveland Arts Prize
Lifetime Achievement metal)

"Our Young Voices is a wonderful opportunity for our youth to express themselves literarily. Such expression is most important to the development of a learned and accomplished community."

Russell Atkins

Russell Atkins is a poet, composer, theorist, editor, and leading literary innovator. He was born on February 25, 1926 in Cleveland, Ohio. He began studying piano at age seven with his mother. From childhood, he exhibited talent in painting, drawing, music, and writing. By age thirteen, he had won several poetry contests. Atkins published his first poem in 1944 in his high school yearbook. With the support of prominent literary figures, Atkins published his poetry in journals and newspapers, including *Experiment* (1947–1951) and the *New York Times* (1951).

Atkins continued his studies of music, performance, and the visual arts through Cleveland College, Cleveland Music School Settlement, Cleveland Institute of Music, Karamu Theatre, and Cleveland School of Art. This musical training is a key to Atkins's poetic style since musical structures are central in his writing.

In 1950, Atkins cofounded what is probably the oldest black-owned literary magazine, *Free Lance*, a publication of avant-garde writing that contributed to the development of New American poetry. He created a style of concrete poetry in which visual presentation of words on the page predominates. He experimented stylistically with the extreme use of the apostrophe, embedding of words within words, and use of continuous words.

In the mid- 1950s, he began utilizing an abstract technique he called "phenomenalism," which juxtaposed unfamiliar and familiar elements. Atkins advocated using the imagination "to exploit range, to create a body of effect, event, colors, characteristics, moods, verbal stresses pushed to a maximum." He did not try to make his work comprehensible to casual readers but strove for dense complexity of meaning.

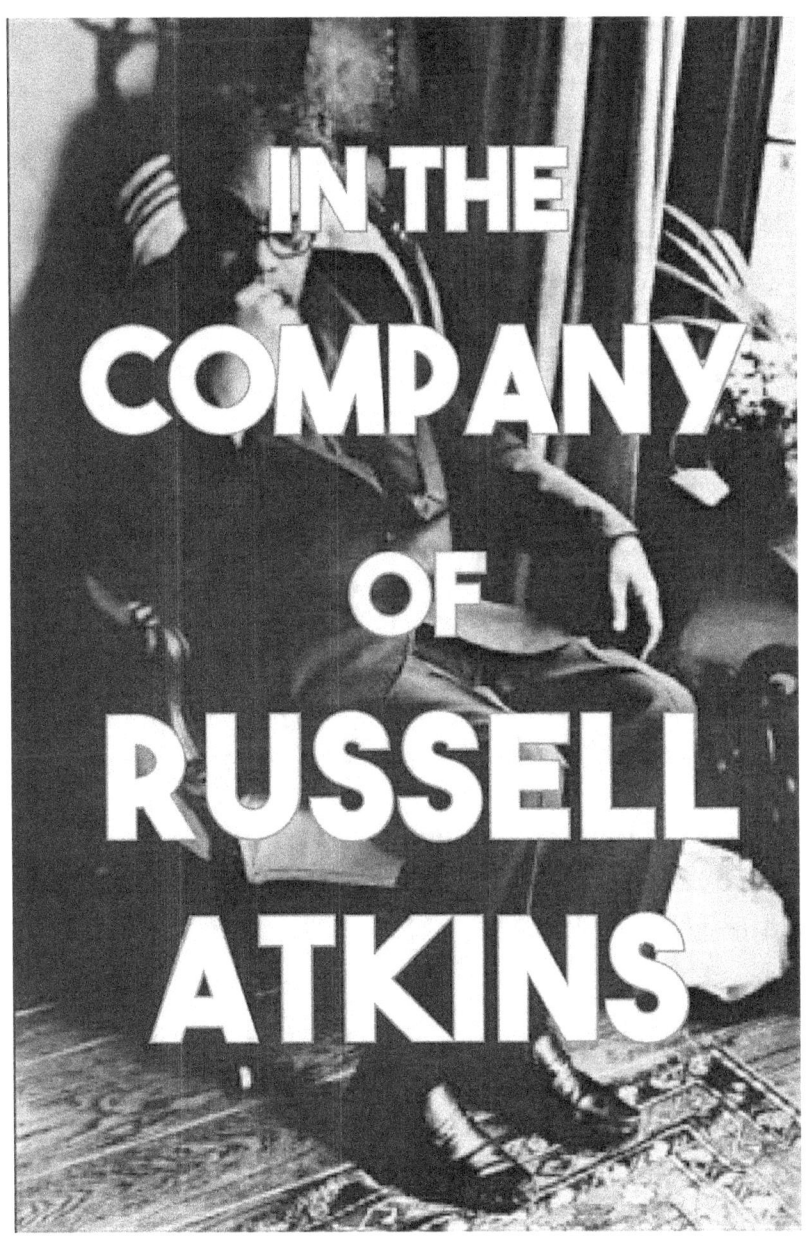

IN THE COMPANY OF RUSSELL ATKINS

While in his 90s Russell Atkins finally has started to get the recognition he so richly deserves. In 2017, an anthology *In The Company of Russell Atkins* was published in his honor. Atkins also, won the Cleveland Arts Prized for Lifetime Achievement and had a portion of Grand Avenue in Cleveland, Ohio renamed to: Russell Atkins Way, Grand Avenue.

(Russell Atkins being awarded "Russell Atkins Way" street sign by Mayor Frank Jackson, standing left, along with original Muntu Poet M.A. Shaheed, standing right)

Carol Shaheed

As a retired history teacher of 36 years and a master's degree in education from Cleveland State University, I am well aware of the importance of our children having the needed skills to read and have their particular voices heard.

By establishing and designing courses such as Black Awareness and Black Biographies, accepted by the state board of education for the East Cleveland school system, allowed my students the opportunity to write and express feeling unique to the black experience.

"Our Young Voices Initiative provides the same opportunities for students to express their uniqueness and I believe that this program allows students to showcase their talents in a productive environment."

Carol Shaheed

Judy Jackson-Winston

JJ Winston has worked in the area of Behavioral Health for over 20 years and is now employed as a Family Court Magistrate Judge in Cleveland, Ohio. JJ Winston is licensed as an Independent Social Worker and Attorney in the state of Ohio.

An avid reader whose hobbies include fishing, watching movies, writing fiction stories and spending time with family and friends. The Anniversary is JJ Winston's first novel.

"I love the fact that our young people have a chance to express themselves in a literary sense and to become a published co-author."

JJ Winston

JJ Winston

The Anniversary

"What do you do when life has you in checkmate?"

Harry Boomer

"My experience in journalism and the media has proven to me how important the ability to express oneself is, both through the spoken and written word. I support the critical aims of Our Young Voices in offering our youth the inspiration, encouragement, and vehicle to make their literary expressions come true as published co-authors."

Harry Boomer

Harry Boomer's broadcasting career began in Washington, D.C., where he was a Disco Jock, an on-air personality, music director, talk show host and served in various other management positions, including two stints as a news director (United Broadcasting and Radio One).

Boomer came to Ohio in 1988 to manage and program WBXT-AM in Canton, Ohio. He also worked in public television at WEAO/WNEO-TV in Kent, Ohio and volunteered at WVIZ-TV 25 Idea Stream in Cleveland.

While covering assignments for WOIO/WUAB on a part-time basis in the early 1990s, he was heard regularly on WCPN-90.3 FM, Cleveland the NPR affiliate, where he served as assistant news director. He was also a reporter, producer and major contributor to NPR. Boomer debuted a statewide news magazine program entitled *Infohio* for the radio station. Boomer took a full time reporter position at channels 19 and 43 WOIO/WUAB and is currently an anchor/reporter and talk show host for the stations. Boomer received the Silver Circle Award in 2015 from the National Academy of Television Arts & Sciences/NATAS, a distinction given for at least 25 years in television.

Boomer is the president of the Greater Cleveland Association of Black Journalist/GCABJ. Twice during Boomer's leadership, the chapter has been named the NABJ Professional Chapter of the Year, most recently in 2016. He is a valued member of the editorial board of Cleveland 19 and CLE 43 in Cleveland, Ohio. He is the executive producer and host of CLE 43 Focus, a weekly, half-hour public affairs show. In 2014 Boomer was named a HistoryMaker and an oral video of his life's story is part of a permanent archive at the Library of Congress. He was named in 2016 as president of the Cleveland Police Athletic League and to the board the Historic League Park in the Hough community of Cleveland. He has served on the boards of the Ohio Associated Press, The Ohio Center for Broadcasting, First Tee Cleveland, the Citizens Committee on AIDS/HIV, the North East Ohio Health Services Board of Directors. He served a member of the Continuing Education Committee at Cleveland State University.

Vince Robinson

Vince Robinson is a Cleveland-based arts advocate involved in a number of pursuits involving media and communication. A 1980 graduate of Kent State University, he initially began as a radio news reporter covering local politics for WKNT-radio. His radio news career included stints at WHLO-AM 640 in Akron, WJMO-1490AM and WERE-1300AM, both in Cleveland. He presently co-hosts 360 Info Network on AM1490-WERE. Additionally, he is the host and co-producer of *Open Door*, a television talk show airing on Cable9 in Summit County, Ohio.

Robinson is also a musician. His group, Vince Robinson & The Jazz Poets, was founded in 1997 with now Cleveland City Councilman Kevin Conwell (drums) and *Horns-N-Things* bassist Derrick James. He plays keys in the Latin soul fusion group *Timbara* and the reggae group *Yardstar*.

In 2016, he and business partner Randy Norfus opened Larchmere Arts, a full-service photography studio, art gallery and performance venue. The business is emerging as a cultural institution in the Larchmere Art district of Cleveland. In addition to music events, cultural activities including lectures and meetings are facilitate in the space. The works of multicultural artists has been featured in the gallery, including paintings, photographs and sculptures.

As a photographer, his work has been shown in galleries and other public spaces. Most recently, a collection of images taken in the West African nation of Ghana was displayed in the Umbajii Gallery at Kent State University. A collection of images of recording artists from several genres was hung in the Shinn House Gallery in Cleveland during the winter of 2017.

Currently, he is serving on a committee to address the needs of African American artists pursuing funding by Cuyahoga Arts and Culture for individual artist grants. He will also be serving on the board of Heights Arts, a non-profit organization serving the arts community of Cleveland Heights, Ohio.

He is a published author, having completed his first book "*Got Words?*" (Parablist Publishing House) in 2015. In partnership with Uptown Media Joint Ventures, his publishing imprint, Sankofa Freedom Press, launched in 2017.

"Our Young Voices is a great opportunity to give inspiration to our young people by celebrating their literary expressions."

Vince Robinson

The Pass It Down Initiative

The Pass It Down Initiative is the brain child of Bryant Wilkerson, aka "B Real tha Poet." This initiative seeks to promote positive outlook and inspiration to youth in the community.

The outreach includes mentoring, job skills training, and literary expression.

When I was 12, leaving the 6th grade, my classmates and I sang, "I BELIEVE THE CHILDREN ARE THE FUTURE." I had no clue what I wanted to do or be but I believed in that song. With that belief I entered the 7th grade, a new school, and was introduced to teenage situations.

I did not have good male/fatherly guidance and I made some horrible decisions. Those decisions lead to a rough life. Therefore, when I see children in need of good guidance I lend my life experiences not just in words but actions as well.

We can talk about our problems complain about our problems but at the end of the day it's on us to change our problems - just like when I was 12 and innocent singing, "I BELIEVE THE CHILDREN ARE THE FUTURE."

I still believe this to be true and this is the reason OUR YOUNG VOICES must be heard, must be shared, must be nurtured, and must be respected!

Bryant Wilkerson
Cleveland, Ohio

2018
Our Young Voices
My Dream Contributors
Cleveland, Ohio

Amya

Christian

Crieg

D.J.

Dewayne

Gregory

Jareese

Kamia

Lawrence

Mikiara

Shanae

Tavonn

Our Dreams Cleveland 2018

Amya

known as flower cake. She is five years old. She will be starting kindergarten this year, 2018. She wants to be a fashion designer because she likes to create dresses.

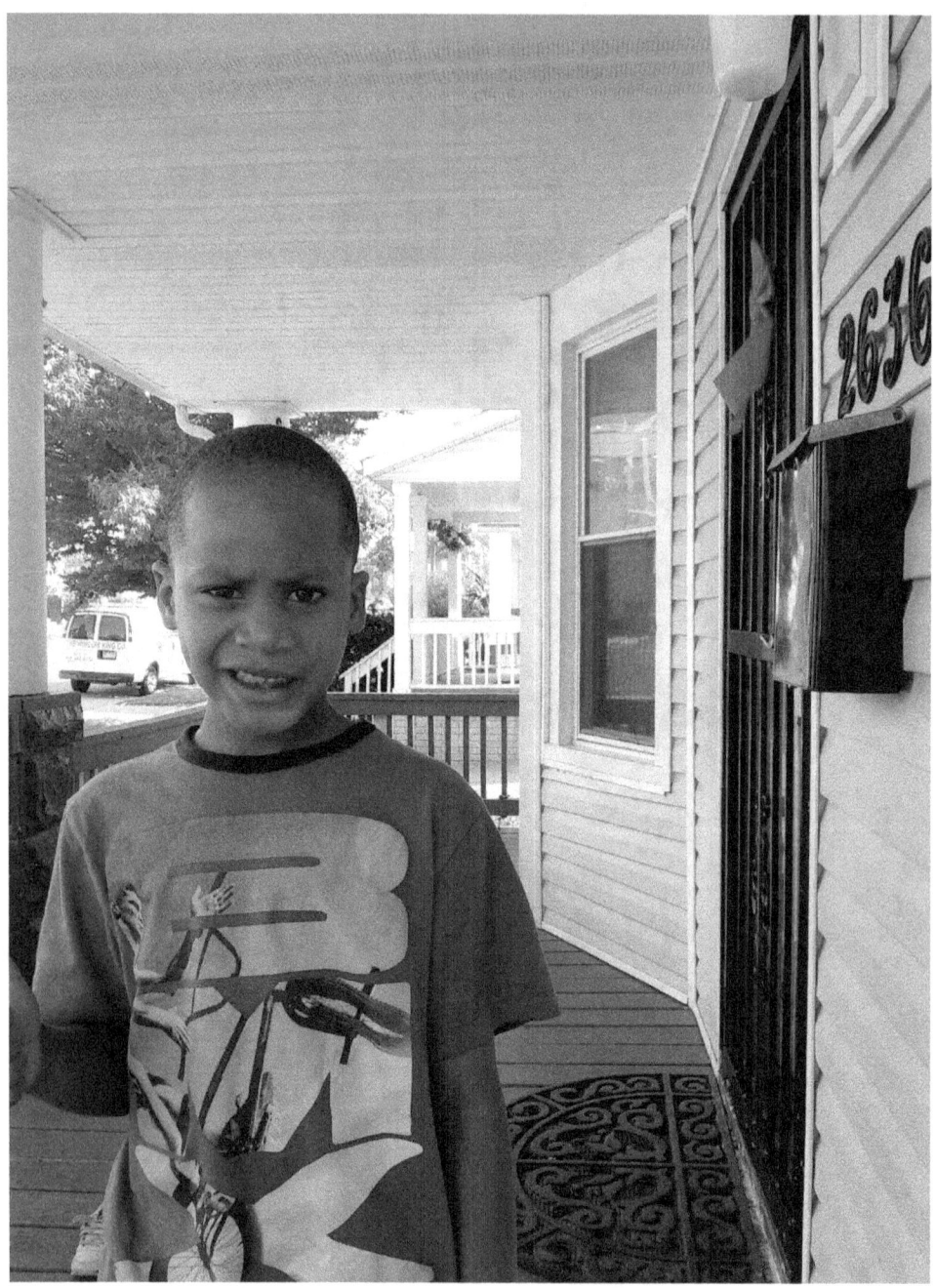

Our Dreams Cleveland 2018

Christian

is 6 years old. He is in the second grade. When he grows up he would like to become a police officer so he can arrest lots of bad people.

Our Dreams Cleveland 2018

Creig

is a 17 year old young man, who is currently attending high school. He is in the 11th grade. He wants to become a police officer once school is over. He enjoys the idea of enforcing "law and order." Someday he wants to help with protecting the community.

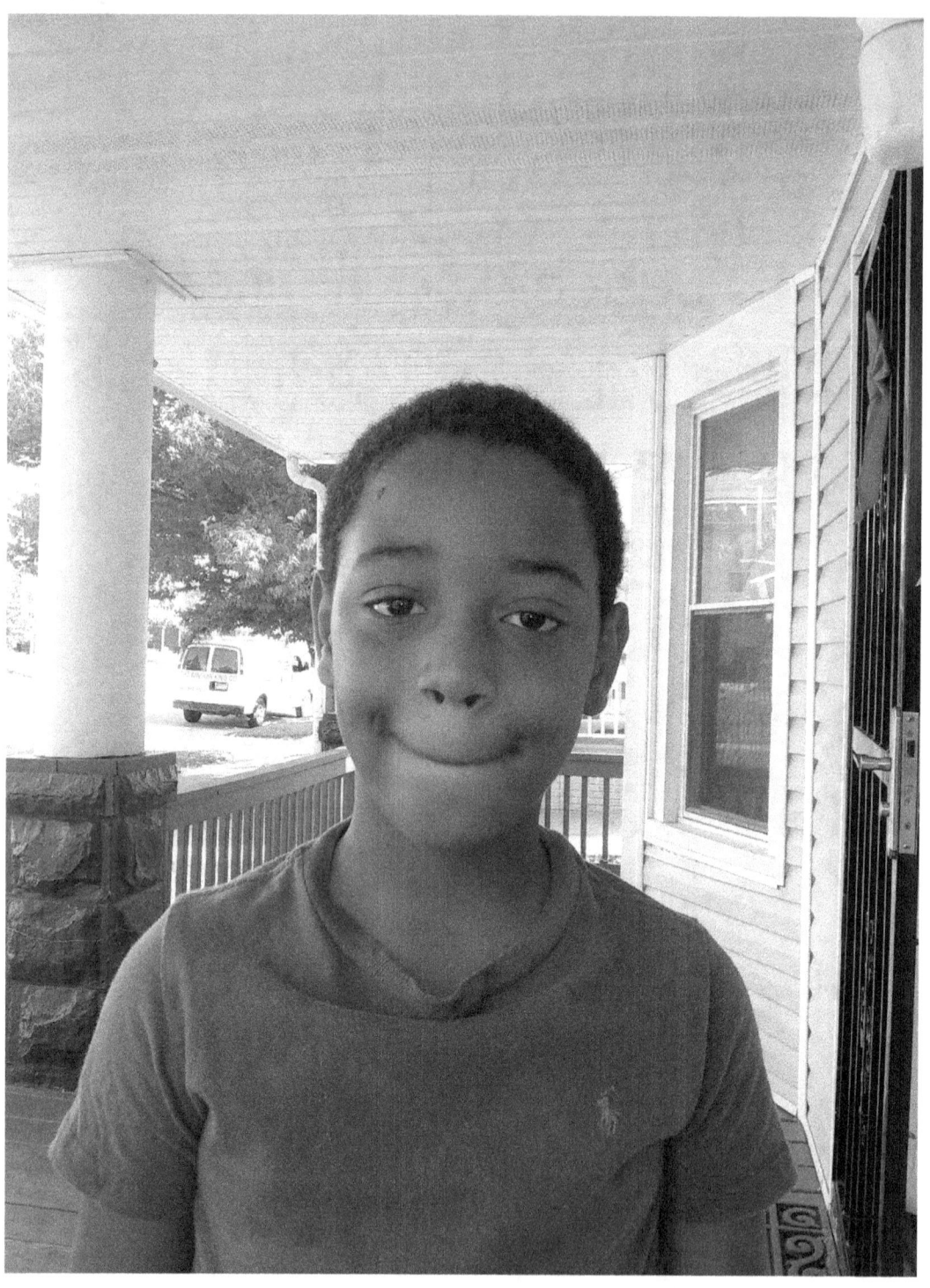

Our Dreams Cleveland 2018

Darnell

known as D.J. He is 8 years old. He's currently in the 3rd grade. When he get all grown up, he wants to become a NFL player. He wants to be a running back because he likes to run.

Our Dreams Cleveland 2018

Dewayne

is 7 years old. He is in the first grade. He wants to be a Dad someday. He has great memories of his dad watching him grow up. And now he wants to repeat the same pattern someday with his children.

Our Dreams Cleveland 2018

Gregory

is 15 years old. He wants to become a mechanic. The high school he currently attends has a program for that field that he will be joining. He likes to work on cars and motor cycles.

Jareese

known as Reese. He is eight
years old. Currently in the third
grade. He wants to become a
fire fighter. He likes to put out
fires and rescue people from
danger.

Our Dreams Cleveland 2018

Kamia

whose nickname is Mia. She is nine years old and currently in the third grade. She would like to be a singer one day. She sings gospel songs every Sunday, and she likes to go to church.

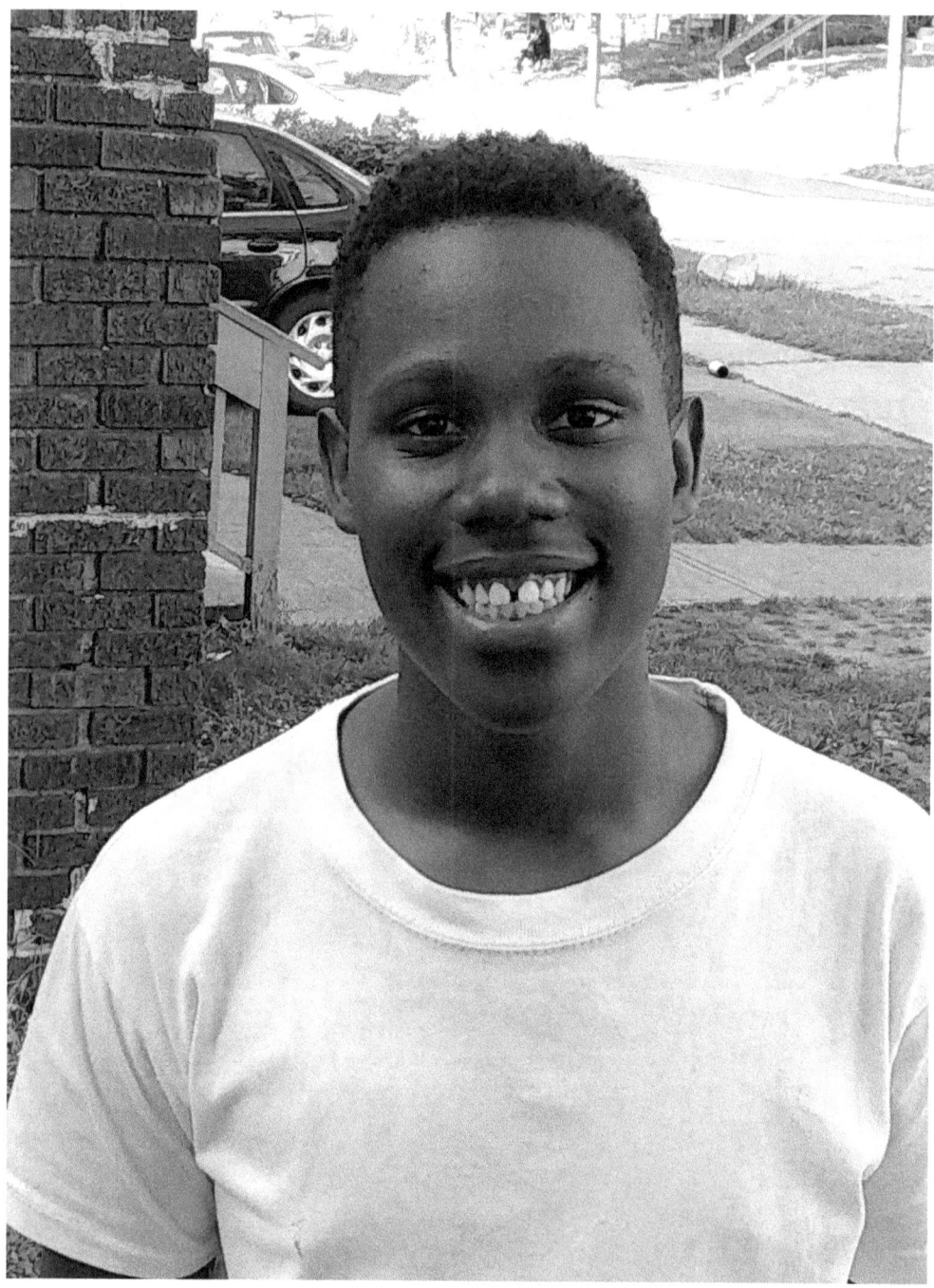

Lawrence

is 15 years old. He is currently attending high school going to the 10th grade. He wants to become a EMS driver someday. He enjoys different sceneries and helping people in many different kinds of emergencies.

Our Dreams Cleveland 2018

Mikiara

known as Ke-ke. She is 12 years old. Currently in the eighth grade. She wants to become an owner of a hair salon because she loves styling hair.

Our Dreams Cleveland 2018

Shanae

she is 15 years old. She loves to sing and dance. Singing is one of the main things she wants to make a career out of. She attends the School of Arts, and has been in three different choirs. If music doesn't work, she would like to help girls that have been traumatized sexually, abandoned, or otherwise abused. She wants to help young girls grow so that they can be prepared for adult life.

Our Dreams Cleveland 2018

Tavonn

known as Tay . He is 13 years old. He is in the seventh grade. He would love to become a football player. The position he wants to play is wide receiver or running back. He loves being a team player.

UNIVERSAL PROSPERITY

THE PRIDE IN AUTHORSHIP INITIATIVE

Our Young Voices *Flashback*

The Spoken Word Cafe

Patrick Henry School
Cleveland, Ohio

The Spoken Word Cafe was held Thursday, November 10, 2016 at the Patrick Henry School. The event was supported by City of Cleveland Councilman, Kevin Conwell; Mrs. Yvonne Conwell, Cuyahoga County Council Representative; Universal Prosperity, Uptown Media Joint Ventures, along with many others.

The main attraction was all the young Spoken Word artists who all were eighth grade students. The various renditions were performed in spirited and eloquent fashions.

The students were joined by various staff in poetic expressions, including Ms. B. Anderson, the Aspiring Principal, along with other staff members.

Other highlights included an upbeat musical presentation by Kevin Conwell and the Footprints Band. Also, uplifting statements were made by various Patrick Henry staff including: Principal, Mrs. M. Martin; Aspiring Principal, Ms. B. Anderson; Assistant Principal, Mr. R. Shaw; and Dean of Engagement, Mr. M. Jester.

This publication certainly is another representation of the dedication to inspiring our youth and service in the community.

Our Dreams Cleveland 2018

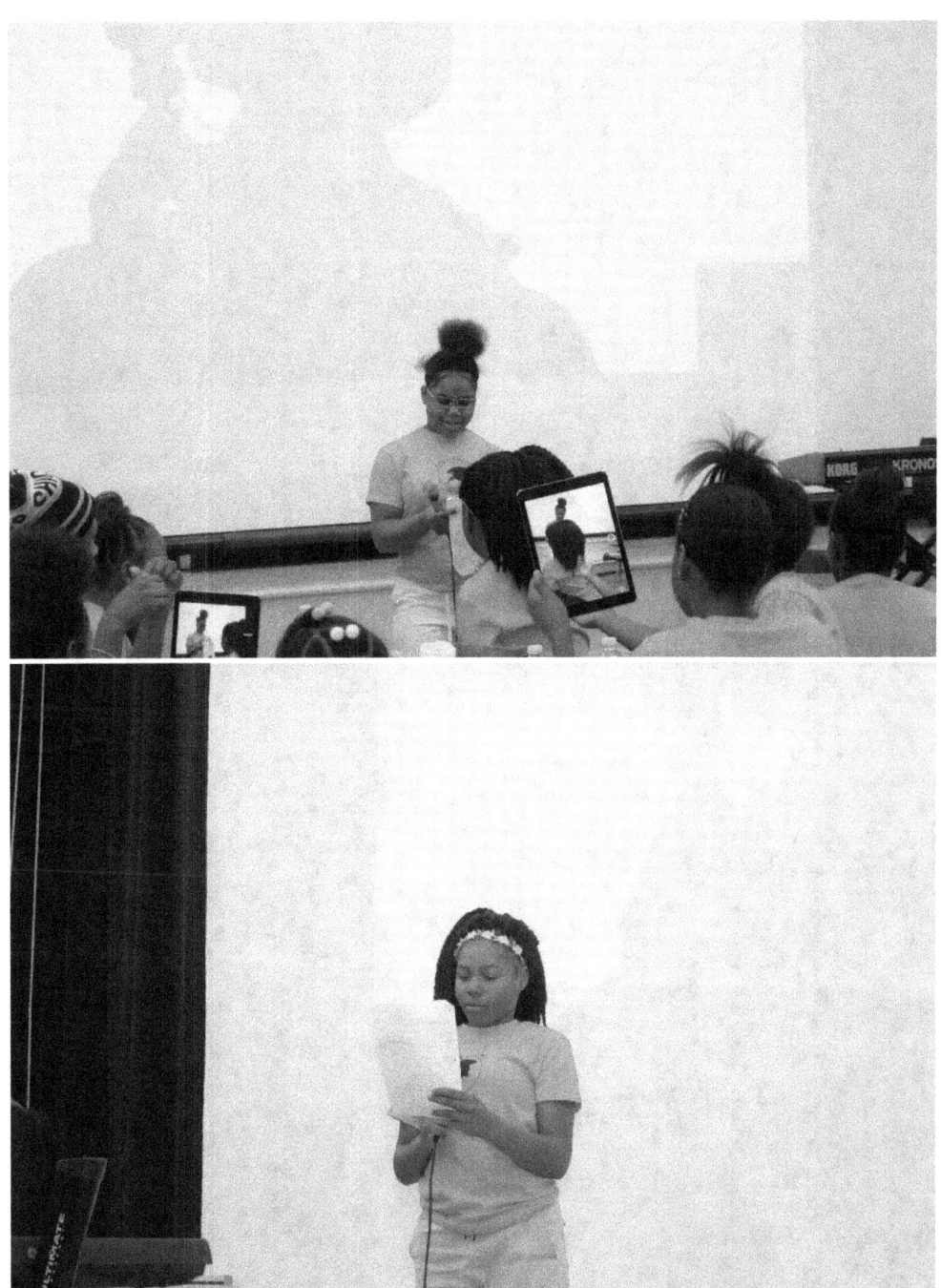

Our Young Voices

Our Dreams Cleveland 2018

Our Young Voices

Coalition For A Better Life, Peace In The Hood

Amir El-Hajj Khalid A. Samad

El Hajj Amir Khalid A. Samad is an internationally known and recognized community activist and leader who formerly served as the Assistant to the Public Safety Director for the City of Cleveland for youth gang intervention. He has also served as a Gang Prevention and Investigative Specialist for the Cleveland Board of Education Gang Task Force. In addition, he is Chief Executive Officer and Co-Founder of Coalition for A Better Life, dba Peace in the Hood, Inc., an organization dedicated to Peace, Justice and Empowerment and also serves as a spokesperson for the International (Formerly National) Council for Urban (Formations) Peace, Justice and Empowerment.

As an internationally acclaimed specialist on urban violence, youth empowerment and gang intervention, Amir Samad has lectured throughout the nation and has appeared on national radio and television shows such as Tavis Smiley, Nightline, Keeping It Real with Rev. Al Sharpton, The Warren Ballentine Show and PBS as a leading authority on these issues. He has served as a convener for the International Council (formerly National Council) Urban (Formations) Peace and Justice Leadership Summits.

In 1987, Khalid Samad, the late Omar Ali-Bey and other community leaders formed The Coalition For A Better Life which addressed the myriad of challenges facing urban America: racism, drugs, gang violence, police corruption, miseducation and an absence of leadership just to name a few. This unified coalition of faith and community based groups involved Muslims, Christians, Jews, Hebrew Israelites , liberals, conservatives, civil rights activists, and community activists, as well as cultural nationalists. This rainbow coalition was inclusive of all ethnic groups and nationalities. This level of cooperation, under Muslim Leadership, was uunprecedented in America given this country's history of inter-religious relations. The Coalition was recognized as a national model for crime prevention and intervention.

The Coalition For A Better Life designed and implemented five monumental projects that were nationally acclaimed. These projects were: 1) Community Empowerment Drug Patrols (which were 24 hours a day, 7 days a week and involved street engagement of violent drug dealers as well as assisting them to cross over into productive life styles by dealing with dealer addiction issues; 2) Rites of Passage, 3) Mentoring (Project A.D.A.M.), 4) Entrepreneurship (Project Ujima) and 5) Cultural Empowerment (Hip Hop exchange which included such nationally known rap artists as Public Enemy, and X-Clan as well as nationally known spoken word artists, The Last Poets). These initiatives together formed Cleveland's first *Community Empowerment*

Project. The notorious King Kennedy Housing Estates was averaging 3 homicides and shootings a week during this time. The efforts of The Coalition for a Better Life sparked a multimillion dollar infusion of improvements and services into King Kennedy and throughout the other housing estates in Cleveland.

Khalid A. Samad is a leading authority on cross-cultural relations, one of the most important religious and cultural diversity issues of our time. He has worked as a member of the City of Cleveland's Arab-American Concerns Committee, established after several robberies and shootings took place in Arab-American owned stores.

In December of 2008, Amir Samad was asked to be one of the panelists in Washington, D.C. at a youth violence summit sponsored by Rep. Bobby Scott of Virginia. On May 7, 2009, he again spoke on youth violence at the Youth Promise Act Day on the Hill. In 2008, 100 Black Men honored (Khalid Samad) as one of the Five Outstanding Cleveland Leaders.

On September 17, 2011, he spoke at a workshop during the Congressional Black Caucus Weekend. In 2012, he was named as one of the Community Heroes by the Plain Dealer for his work in the community. In 2012, he also received the Community Hero Award, North Coast Nurses Association. In 2016, he was inducted into the Cleveland International Hall of Fame, one of 7 inductees out of over 150 nominees. He was also honored by Cleveland City Council in 2016 for his over 41 years of service to the community.

Brother Samad has continued his tireless work on behalf of the youth of Cleveland, speaking in the schools, community and religious institutions, always having time to just talk to them and provide a listening ear and guidance with their problems. He continues to be in demand as a trainer for police, school officials, and the community in issues of gang prevention and intervention and non-violent crisis intervention and mediation. He has continued to embody and work for the principles of Peace in the Hood in his daily life: Peace, Justice and Empowerment.

"The Coalition for a Better Life, Peace in the Hood is happy and enthusiastic to lend support to the Our Young Voices Initiative. Inspiring our young people must be a priority in these turbulent times."

Khalid Samad

This is the symbol for the principle of Umoja (Unity in the Community)

We hope you enjoyed seeing these pictures! We had a great time! We hope to see everyone out for our next event!

Take the Book Phone Challenge!

Smart is Cool!

Round 1
Boxing. Fitness. Life.

Boxer and ordained minister the Rev. Morris Eason has a passion for helping both kids and adults overcome life's many struggles through a "proven regimen of boxing, training and life coaching." He wholeheartedly supports the Our Young Voices Initiative.

"Morris Eason, a former boxer who once beat "Boom Boom" Mancini. Eason, who often competes in regional tough-man contests, combines the manners of a church deacon -- he's an ordained minister -- with the look of a hit man: bald head, bulging pecs, jaw as square as a sock hop."

Scene Magazine, October 23, 2002

ROUND 1 MINISTRIES
Motivational Speaking, Fitness & Life Coaching

8490 Kinsman road, Novelty, Ohio 44072 • **P.O. Box 23474** • Chagrin Falls, OH 44022
P 216.978.6919 • P 440-708 4376 • morris.eason@yahoo.com

Hello,
My Name is Rev. Morris Eason, former Regional Toughman Champion
and World Toughman Sweet 16 Finalist. My passion in life is helping
kids and families to overcome life's many struggles. Through a
proven regimen of boxing, training and life coaching, I can help.
If you want to travel down a new path, please contact me
right away!

Motivational Speaking

My motivational speeches are geared to inspire audience members to make a
change in their lives. Through my personal stories, derived from over 30 years
of being in the "Ring," I hope everyone will feel my passion and energy and
leave empowered to impact their lives in a positive manner. My fees start at
$500 for an event, plus expenses.

One-On-One and Group Fitness Training

There is no other workout like that of a boxer. Minute for minute, a boxer's
routine teaches agility, endurance, conditioning and coordination. I conduct
daily one hour group boxing fitness sessions consisting of 4 people in a class
in addition to scheduled private one-on-one individual lessons. My fees are
$15 for the group and $50 for individual sessions.

Counseling: Bullying, Self Esteem, Confidence & Drug Addiction

Bullying, face to face as well as on the internet, and the resulting emotional
distress, has become one of the most prevalent problems in today's schools.
Kids looking to cope with pressures and family issues often believe that drugs or
alcohol will medicate that pain but they soon learn its not the answer. My unique
method of combining training, self confidence and personal communication has
proven to help these youngsters pull their lives back together. Initial sessions are
free. Thereafter, individual sessions are $50 per hour.

Prison Ministry

A record number of kids and young adults are being incarcerated into our
prison systems. Often these inmates lose hope and harden their hearts.
Through my weekly visits, I have been able to give them a renewed hope and
a purpose for living again. Many stays in jail are temporary and these young
lives need a ray of hope in dealing with their futures. That's exactly what I do.
My services are free. Donations are appreciated.

ROUND 1
Boxing. Fitness. Life.

Our Dreams Cleveland 2018

UNIVERSAL
PROSPERITY

Promoting Business
and Social Unity

NON SECTARIAN
NON POLITICAL

Our Young Voices

Our Young Voices

2018

Our Dreams

Cleveland, Ohio

UPTOWN
MEDIA JOINT VENTURES
PUBLISHING

www.ingramcontent.com/pod-product-compliance
Lightning Source LLC
Chambersburg PA
CBHW082050220626
47052CB00006B/1203